Railways & Recollections 19

Contents

© Chris Harris 2014

Photographs by Ray Ruffell © The NOSTALGIA Collection archive, unless otherwise credited

All rights reserved. No part of this publication may be reproduced, stored in a retrieval system or transmitted, in any form or by any means, electronic, mechanical, photocopying, recording or otherwise, without prior permission in writing from Silver Link Publishing Ltd.

First published in 2014

British Library Cataloguing in Publication Data

A catalogue record for this book is available from the British Library.

ISBN 978 1 85794 430 3

Silver Link Publishing Ltd
The Trundle
Ringstead Road
Great Addington
Kettering
Northants NN14 4BW

Tel/Fax: 01536 330588
email: sales@nostalgiacollection.com
Website: www.nostalgiacollection.com

Printed and bound in the Czech Republic

Frontispiece: **WORKINGTON** The two-car diesel multiple unit (DMU) forming the 0846 Whitehaven to Carlisle service calls at the spacious Workington station on Monday 11 April 1983. A Travelling Post Office carriage stands between two BR Standard Mark 1 BGs on one of the centre non-platform lines. During 2012 Workington station benefited from a £200,000 refurbishment scheme.

Acknowledgements

It would not have been possible to produce this book without making use of two very extensive photographic collections. Many of the illustrations started in the camera of the late Ray Ruffell. Ray was a railwayman by profession, but his interest in transport went far beyond his day-to-day work. In his off-duty time he travelled widely, and in so doing created an extensive photographic record of the railway system during a period when great change was under way. Other photographs in this volume were taken by Brian Jackson, a fellow transport historian who has also travelled extensively across the UK armed with his camera to record the ever-changing transport scene. My warm thanks to Brian for allowing me to use some of the photographs he took during 1983.

Many scenes that were everyday and commonplace when Ray or Brian photographed them have now been swept away for ever, and the memories captured on film, precious at the time, are now beyond price. It is pleasing to record that the late Ray Ruffell's collection of photographs has been kept complete and is now in the safe keeping of *The NOSTALGIA Collection*, forming an important part of the company's photographic archives.

I would like to say a sincere thank you to the team at *The NOSTALGIA Collection* for inviting me to write this book. The cheerful and willing help I have received from Peter Townsend, Will Adams and David Walshaw has been very much appreciated, and I feel deeply honoured to work with such kind people.

I hope that you will enjoy this look back at 1983 and will want to sample more years in the 'Railways & Recollections' series.

Introduction: The year of the Serpell Report – and breakfast television

On Thursday 20 January 1983 the publication of the Serpell Committee Report caused something of a stir among those who cared about the future of public transport in Britain. The Committee had been set up by the Government in May 1982 with a brief 'to examine the future of the railway and associated operations … and to report on alternative policies … designed to secure improved financial results'. The Report included maps illustrating a number of possible options, and Option A, purporting to be the commercial railway, showed only 1,630 route miles open for passenger traffic – less than 20% of the network then in operation. Not surprisingly there was a huge furore; under the onslaught of this opposition, and probably not wishing to prolong a political storm with a general election in the offing, the Government quietly put aside the Serpell Report.

A positive event was the commencement of electric services between Moorgate/St Pancras and Bedford during the early summer after industrial relations problems arising from the introduction of driver-only operation had finally been resolved. Because of this dispute, some of the new trains built for the route had stood idle for more than a year – to the displeasure of customers who had to continue to travel in diesel multiple units dating from 1959 until agreement was reached to operate the new trains. Meanwhile,

on the East Coast Main Line the National Coal Board had financed a new 14.5-mile section of track from Templehurst (south of Selby) to Colton (on the Leeds-York line), allowing the Selby coalfield to be further exploited without affecting the operation of this main line. In fact, the new alignment was suitable for 125mph running, and East Coast express services no longer had to contend with the speed limits imposed by the curves and swing bridge at Selby.

In September 1983 Robert Reid became Chairman of British Rail, and quickly expressed his intention that the railway should become more commercially led.

The breaking news of the Serpell Report may have been one of the first topics that many people watched on breakfast television. The BBC launched *Breakfast Time* on Monday 17 January; ITV was not far behind – TV-am's *Good Morning Britain* came to our screens on Tuesday 1 February.

Shocking news during February was the discovery of dismembered remains of a number of young men at a property occupied by Dennis Nilsen in North London; he subsequently admitted killing 15 men and following his trial was jailed for life in November.

On the roads, the wearing of seat belts became compulsory for car-drivers and front-seat passengers, while wheel clamps

started to be used on illegally parked vehicles. Happier news for motorists was the opening in November of the 37-mile M54 motorway linking the M6 with the new town of Telford and with Wellington. Prefix letters for car registrations, appropriately starting with A, commenced in August 1983.

In the general election on Thursday 9 June, the Conservatives were returned with a majority of 144 seats (42% of votes cast).

Sadly the year ended on a note of violence when a Provisional IRA car bomb outside Harrods in London killed six people and injured a further 90; another bomb exploded in London's Oxford Street on Christmas Day, but fortunately without casualties.

1983 was the year when the pound in your pocket, whatever the effects of inflation, became slightly heavier to carry – the pound coin was introduced as a replacement for the pound note. For those who enjoyed spending their leisure time at the cinema, new releases included *Yentl* and *Educating Rita*.

Please join me as we take a trip around the railway network and rekindle memories of 1983…

Chris Harris
Poole, Dorset

Around London and the South East

WHITECHAPEL A London Transport District Line train bound for Upminster is seen entering Whitechapel station in East London on Wednesday 11 May 1983. The train is formed of D78 stock, which was introduced on the District Line from January 1980 onwards, and was designed with single-leaf doorways of a narrower width than was usual for Underground stock. Beneath these platforms, what was then the East London Line passes beneath at right angles in a deeper cutting, with steps down to interchange platforms; in the 21st century this line has become part of the London Overground system, which, after the opening of the link between Queens Road Peckham and Surrey Quays in December 2012, now forms part of an 'outer circle' rail route around London. The importance of Whitechapel as an interchange station will further increase with the projected opening of the deep-level Crossrail platforms in 2018; the existing Whitechapel Road entrance to the station will be retained.

PARK ROYAL The British Rail Western Region line from Paddington to High Wycombe can be seen on the right of this photograph, also taken on Wednesday 11 May; on the left is the West Ruislip branch of London Transport's Central Line, which was opened between North Acton and Greenford on 30 June 1947 and extended onwards to West Ruislip the following year. The eight-car train is made up of 1962 tube stock, which continued to provide services on the Central Line until it was replaced by new trains from 1993 onwards; the last 1962 stock train ran on the Central Line in early 1995. The overbridge carries the Uxbridge branch of the Piccadilly Line, which has a station at Park Royal a short distance away, but as there is now no station on the Central Line at this location (between North Acton and Hanger Lane) interchange between the two lines is not possible; when the Central Line service commenced in 1947 the GWR Park Royal West Halt, which dated from 1932, was closed.

Below: **WATERLOO** On Sunday 20 May new Class 455 unit No 5820 (on the left) had been allocated to the 'Kingston roundabout' circular route when photographed in the 'North' platforms at Waterloo. The arrival of the Class 455 units allowed the Class 508 units to be transferred to Merseyside. The 508s had been introduced from 1980, but they had been less than successful on the Southern, and moreover were not compatible with any of the Region's other stock. They were, however, almost identical to the Class 507 units operated on Merseyside, and the transfer northwards of most of this stock was completed in December 1984. Still on the Southern at this time, No 508029, on the right, will form the next departure to Windsor & Eton Riverside. This part of Waterloo station was demolished in the early 1990s to allow the Eurostar terminal to be built.

Above: **WATERLOO** Three generations of Southern Region suburban stock are illustrated in this photograph taken on Thursday 30 June. On the left, 4SUB unit No 4279 was one of the decreasing number of these trains still active in 1983. By early August all 4SUB workings on timetabled services at Waterloo had ceased, but No 4279 was then used on Central section services, and together with sister unit No 4754 operated the final timetabled 4SUB workings in public service on Tuesday 6 September 1983. At the next platform 4EPB unit No 5125 looks quite similar to the 4SUB; as well as being equipped with electro-pneumatic brakes, the cabs and front ends were redesigned for these units, and while roller-blind headcode panels were included (as opposed to stencils), in some ways they lacked the character of the older SUB units. On the right, Class 455 unit No 5810 represents the latest Southern suburban stock in 1983. The first units of this type entered passenger service from 28 March of that year, and the continuing deliveries were enabling the progressive withdrawal of the remaining 4SUB units.

WATERLOO SOUTH SIDINGS On Thursday 21 April new Class 455 unit No 5803 is berthed in the sidings on the south side of the running lines at the approach to Waterloo station; at this time training runs with these units ran as empty stock between Waterloo and Shepperton on Tuesdays, Thursdays and Saturdays. The Necropolis station, from which funeral trains had operated to the large cemetery at Brookwood, had been located in the area to the right of this photograph. Originally opened in 1854, the Necropolis station had been rebuilt by the LSWR in 1902, but was destroyed in an air raid during the night of 16 April 1941 and not rebuilt, the site later being occupied by prefabricated office buildings.

CLAPHAM YARD A train of cement tanks is headed by electro-diesel locomotive No 73114 on Tuesday 15 March. These versatile locomotives could operate using the third-rail traction supply at 1,600hp, or from an auxiliary diesel generator at a lower 600hp. Originally numbered E6020, No 73114 had entered service in February 1966. Diesel-electric locomotive No 33101, just visible in the right foreground, was built by the Birmingham Railway Carriage & Wagon Company as No D6511 and entered service in May 1960. It was fitted for push-pull operation in June 1967, and for a number of years was used mainly on passenger services between Bournemouth and Weymouth. It was withdrawn in May 1993 and subsequently scrapped. A variety of passenger stock can be seen in the yard in the background.

SHEPPERTON The branch line from the Kingston loop to Shepperton is just over 6 miles long and was opened in November 1864. There were ambitions that the line would be continued to Chertsey, and Shepperton was designed in the manner of a through station with the buildings beside what would have been the down platform, but the extension was never proceeded with. The line was electrified in January 1916, and when this photograph was taken on Saturday 21 May 1983 new Class 455 unit No 5825 waits in the station to form the 0940 service to Waterloo. The station buildings, in an attractive Italianate style and built by John Aird & Son with the line, are partly visible on the left; the station was subsequently completely rebuilt in 1988 as part of a development that included new office accommodation.

EFFINGHAM JUNCTION This station, near the junction of the Leatherhead to Guildford line and the so-called Guildford 'new' line via Cobham, was opened in July 1888. Almost 95 years later, on Sunday 19 June 1983, Class 455 unit No 5814 has emerged from the sidings into the up platform to form the 1009 service to Waterloo. The scene here has been considerably changed in the recent past. New waiting shelters have replaced the traditional-style platform buildings seen in the photograph, while the wooden booking office – at footbridge level and out of sight to the left of this view – has been replaced by a modern brick and flint station building formally opened on Thursday 31 May 2012. Overall passenger access has been improved by the rebuilding and modernisation, which involved a partnership between the Department for Transport, South West Trains and Network Rail.

Right: **WOKING** Train journeys on Sundays are sometimes subject to diversions in order to allow essential engineering work to take place on track, signalling or other structures. On Sunday 13 March 1983 passengers travelling between Reading and Gatwick Airport were diverted via Woking instead of taking the usual route through North Camp. Their train is a three-car Class 119 DMU built by the Gloucester Railway Carriage & Wagon Company in 1958. These units were originally built to operate on quite long cross-country services; the Driving Motor Brake Composite (furthest from the camera in this view) incorporated a large van area, while the trailer car in the centre of the unit included a small buffet.

Thus in the early 1980s some of these units were considered ideal for the Reading to Gatwick Airport service, with the large van space and the by then long-disused buffet being designated and labelled as passenger luggage stowage areas. All of the Class 119 units had been withdrawn from service by the mid-1990s.

Left: **ASCOT** Sporting events often led to the operation of special trains. On Thursday 16 June 1983 this rake of air-conditioned stock hauled by Class 47 No 47545 had departed from Swansea at 0937 to bring punters from South Wales to the race meeting at Royal Ascot. Built as No D1646, the locomotive was renumbered under the TOPS system. The train is using the rather unusual London-bound platform at Ascot, which consists of a single track through the station with platform faces on both sides. Race meetings, and particularly Royal Ascot in June, continue to provide additional traffic for Ascot station, which retains much of its traditional atmosphere.

Chester and in North Wales. The last was withdrawn from normal passenger service in February 1983, but the unit seen here at Guildford on Tuesday 22 March had been removed from the passenger fleet in 1970 for conversion to departmental use. Converted to become 'Laboratory Coach No 5', this unit was used by the BR Research Division at Derby as a track-recording unit – in this guise it was used for longer than it had been in passenger service, eventually being sent for scrap in 1991. When photographed the unit was awaiting clearance to proceed to Woking in order to make trips over the line between there and Basingstoke. Note the wording on the car end, drawing attention to the care that needed to be taken to protect the equipment being carried.

Above: **GUILDFORD** The early-morning Sabbath calm is interrupted on Sunday 22 May when the 0600 ex-Petersfield van train arrives at Guildford headed by Class 50 diesel locomotive No 50028. Built by English Electric Vulcan Foundry and entering service as No D428 on the London Midland Region in June 1968, No 50028 was transferred to the Western Region in May 1974, and was given the name *Tiger* four years later. Withdrawal came in February 1991, and the locomotive was cut up by Coopers Metals at Old Oak Common in July of that year.

Right: **GUILDFORD** As part of the BR Modernisation Plan, Park Royal Vehicles Limited gained a contract to supply 20 two-car DMUs powered by AEC engines with mechanical transmission. These units entered traffic in November 1957 and were of distinctive appearance; they were used mainly on services around

SOUTHAMPTON CENTRAL

Trains from London Waterloo to Southampton, Bournemouth and Weymouth have to pass through the 528-yard tunnel under the city before arriving at Southampton Central station. The tunnel dates from 1847, and by the early 1980s its condition was causing concern. It was necessary to reline it, and to replace the original brick base of the structure with a much deeper concrete base. Because of the density of traffic on the line, it was impractical to close the tunnel except for short periods, so the contractors – Edmund Nuttall – had to carry out this work while the trains were still running. Accordingly, additional crossovers were laid at each end of the tunnel to facilitate single-line working, which was brought into operation in the spring of 1983 so that repairs could commence.

The contractors laid their own narrow-gauge railway to transport the necessary materials into the tunnel from a point just east of Southampton Central station; these trains were also used to remove debris and spoil from the work site. These photographs were taken on Friday 20 May and illustrate the narrow-gauge railway in use. In the second picture, an unidentified Class 47 diesel-electric passes with a train of oil tanks on the single line available for normal rail traffic. The renovation was completed and the tunnel returned to normal working on 8 July 1985, and it is very much to the credit of all concerned that this major project on a busy main line was carried out with minimal effects on train services.

BOTLEY On the line from Fareham to Eastleigh, Botley station opened in February 1842, and in 1863 became the junction for the short branch line to Bishop's Waltham. The branch closed to passengers in January 1933, but remained open for goods traffic until April 1962. The stub of the old branch line can be seen in the background of the photograph to the right of the main running lines, occupied by a Foster Yeoman stone and aggregate terminal connected by overhead conveyor to the main plant on the other side of the line. These photographs were taken on Saturday 16 July 1983 looking towards Eastleigh; the main station building, which previously stood on the Eastleigh-bound platform, has been replaced by a small metal shelter, although the wooden shelter on the island platform survives from the original buildings.

In the second photograph, three-car diesel-electric multiple unit (DEMU) No 1401 approaches the station as the 1511 service to Fareham and Portsmouth. It had

started life in 1957 as a two-car unit; the centre trailer is a former 2EPB electric driving trailer that had been converted in 1964 for use in the so-called 'Tadpole' DEMUs used between Reading and Tonbridge. When four of the 'Tadpoles' were disbanded in May 1979 their ex-2EPB driving trailers were reused again to lengthen the four remaining two-car 'Hampshire' units to three cars.

This line was electrified in 1990 as part of the Solent electrification scheme; electric multiple units (EMUs) now provide an hourly through service to London Waterloo and passenger numbers have increased. The shelters on both platforms have been replaced by more modern structures, but Botley station is unstaffed. Concurrently with the electrification, a new station was opened at Hedge End between Botley and Eastleigh.

AMBERLEY Situated between Pulborough and Arundel on the Arun Valley line, Amberley station was opened by the London, Brighton & South Coast Railway in 1863. The first view is looking north towards Pulborough and London Victoria. There is an attractive wooden shelter with a curved corrugated-iron roof on the up platform, while the main station buildings are on the down platform on the right of the photograph. The building ends rather abruptly with a rendered wall at the end nearest the camera – this is where the station house had stood prior to demolition, but fortunately the booking office remains. Notice the very small signal cabin nestling beneath the platform canopy. A signal box had originally been located at the south end of the up platform, but was relocated here in January 1934 as an extension of the booking office. Amberley station serves the villages of Amberley and Houghton Bridge, and for some years the booking office also fulfilled the role of Houghton Bridge Post Office until this very unusual arrangement was ended in 1969.

The interior view shows how the diminutive signal box was connected directly to the booking office with no internal wall or door; the ticket-issuing window is just out of sight immediately to the right of the photograph.

The line through Amberley station was electrified in 1938, and passengers using the station now include visitors to the Amberley Museum located in large chalk quarries nearby.

AMBERLEY MUSEUM The site now occupied by the museum was used as chalk pits and a lime works from the 1840s until the 1960s, and the former course of sidings from the erstwhile goods yard at Amberley station is now the path to enter the museum. Amberley Museum provides 36 acres where visitors can enjoy the industrial heritage of South East England. Transport offerings include a Southdown bus collection and an old-style village garage, together with a superb industrial railway collection. During a visit on Thursday 7 April 1983 Ray Ruffell photographed two examples from the extensive collection of narrow-gauge industrial locomotives. The Hunslet diesel in the first picture was originally fleet number 4 for Thakenham Tiles of Storrington, West Sussex, and dates from 1946. The cab and rear of this locomotive were rebuilt by Thakenham Tiles,

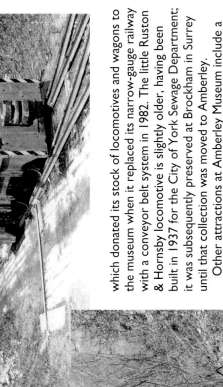

which donated its stock of locomotives and wagons to the museum when it replaced its narrow-gauge railway with a conveyor belt system in 1982. The little Ruston & Hornsby locomotive is slightly older, having been built in 1937 for the City of York Sewage Department; it was subsequently preserved at Brockham in Surrey until that collection was moved to Amberley.

Other attractions at Amberley Museum include a telecommunications exhibition, a typical West Sussex fire station of the 1950s, a museum of roads and road-making, a printing workshop, and a fascinating display of vintage wireless and television sets. Open every day during the West Sussex school Easter and summer holidays, the museum – very conveniently served by rail to Amberley station – is well worth a visit.

1983 Happenings (1)

January

- Publication of Serpell Report considering possible future options for Britain's railway system; alternatives presented include a severe reduction in the network to just 1,630 miles. Report causes furore and is quietly shelved by Government.
- BBC's *Breakfast Time* becomes first breakfast television programme in Britain.
- It is made compulsory for car-drivers and front-seat passengers to wear seat belts.
- EEC Common Fisheries Policy comes into effect.

February

- ITV introduces TV-am.
- Unemployment reaches a record high of 3,224,715.

March

- Compact discs go on sale in UK.
- Austin Maestro is launched.

April

- Thousands of protesters form human chain to object to placing of American nuclear weapons at British military bases.
- Gunmen escape with £7 million from Security Express van in London.
- Vauxhall launches Nova range of saloons and hatchbacks.
- One pound coin is introduced in England and Wales.

May

- Multiple killer Dennis Nilsen arrested in North London.
- Wheel clamps used to combat illegal parking in London.

June

- General election is won by Conservatives with majority of 144 seats; the party's share of popular vote is 42%.
- Michael Foot resigns as leader of Labour Party.
- Roy Jenkins resigns as leader of Social Democratic Party and is succeeded by David Owen.
- National Museum of Photography, Film and Television opens in Bradford.

TONBRIDGE A contrast in 1950s DMUs is illustrated at Tonbridge on Thursday 3 November 1983. On the left, unit No 1006 has arrived as the 1044 service from Hastings to Charing Cross. This is a six-car DEMU of the type designated 6S, the carriages being built on short 56ft 11in underframes; it was built at BR Eastleigh Works and entered service in 1957. These units were especially designed for the Hastings line, and had severe straight sides because of restricted clearances in several tunnels on that route. On the right, mailbags are being loaded into the large brake van of a three-car diesel-mechanical multiple unit built by the Gloucester Railway Carriage & Wagon Company in 1958; this train will form the 1151 service to Reading via Redhill.

MV 'St Catherine' takes to the seas

PORTSMOUTH In 1983 Sealink was still part of British Rail, and ferry services to and from the Isle of Wight were a significant part of the operation. Two routes were provided to the Island from Portsmouth: for foot passengers between Portsmouth Harbour station and Ryde Pier Head, and a car ferry linking Portsmouth with Fishbourne. In 1982 the Portsmouth terminal for this very busy vehicle route had been moved from Broad Street to its present site in Gunwharf Road, and the first of a new generation of ships that were to bring about a huge improvement to this crossing was introduced in the summer of 1983. MV *St Catherine* was built by Robb, Caledon Shipbuilders at Leith with a capacity for 142 cars and 771 passengers (the high passenger capacity was required to cater for coach parties travelling to and from the Isle of Wight). Before taking up her duties MV *St Catherine* underwent trials from Portsmouth, where Ray Ruffell took these photographs on Sunday 26 June; the new ship entered service from Sunday 3 July.

Another new vessel, MV *St Helen*, was introduced on the Portsmouth to Fishbourne route from 28 November 1983. These new ships allowed the withdrawal of MV *Fishbourne* and MV *Camber Queen*, which dated from 1961, while the 1973-built MV *Caedmon* was transferred to join her similar sisters MV *Cuthred* and MV *Cenred* on the Lymington to Yarmouth route.

Sealink was privatised in 1984, and since 1991 the erstwhile Sealink routes to and from the Isle of Wight have traded as Wightlink. MV *St Catherine* served the Portsmouth to Fishbourne route for 26 years until she was withdrawn in 2009. The following year she was sold to Italy-based ferry company Delcomar; she has been renamed GB *Conte* and at the time of writing sails in the warmer waters of the Mediterranean.

Go West, young man

SWINDON The middle years of the 19th century saw the then small market town of Swindon in Wiltshire transformed after the establishment of the railway works; their construction commenced in 1841 and the plant opened in January 1843. By 1900 the works employed more than 12,000 people, and Swindon was regarded as the heart of the Great Western Railway. It was said that during the 1930s Swindon Works was capable of building three locomotives a week; production was later switched to diesel locomotives until new motive power construction at Swindon ceased in 1965, although repairs and carriage and wagon work continued. The outside of the works was photographed on a quiet Sunday afternoon in August 1983; once this entrance would have been alive with hundreds of men either commencing or completing their shifts, but by 1983 the works was a shadow of its former self, and complete closure came in 1986. *Brian Jackson*

SWINDON By the late 1970s it was realised that the 4CEP and 4BEP units built originally for the Southern Region's Kent Coast electrification schemes between 1956 and 1963 were likely to have to remain in service until the end of the 20th century, but the interior appointments of the carriages were felt to be very dated. Following the experimental rebuild of one unit at Eastleigh in 1975, the contract for the refurbishment of the entire 4CEP/4BEP fleet was awarded to Swindon Works in 1979. The project was in full swing during 1983, and here the Driving Motor Open 2nd of unit No 7133 is seen receiving attention – the former van space behind the cab is being converted into a seating area. The refurbished units certainly looked brighter and more modern, but a number of users considered that they had been more spacious and comfortable in their original condition. *Brian Jackson*

TAUNTON On Friday 1 July 1983 Class 50 diesel-electric locomotive No 50015 *Valiant* was photographed from Forty Steps Bridge, west of Taunton station, with an up express. New in April 1968 as No D415, *Valiant* was withdrawn in June 1992 and passed into preservation, now being owned by the Bury Valiant Group and based on the East Lancashire Railway. Fairwater Bridge can be seen in the background, and to the right the 50-foot-tower of Taunton School will be noted. This independent school was founded in 1847, although the Victorian Gothic-style buildings on the current site date from the 1870s and are Grade 2 listed. *Brian Jackson*

TAUNTON Moving now to Fairwater Bridge, this photograph was taken on the same day as Class 50 No 50038 *Formidable* left Taunton with a down train, passing the extensive grounds of Taunton School. New in September 1968 as No D438, *Formidable* was in service for 20 years, being withdrawn in September 1988 and subsequently scrapped. The Class 50 locomotives were originally built to haul trains on the London Midland Region's West Coast Main Line between Crewe and Glasgow, and when this route was electrified in 1974 they were transferred to the Western Region. No fewer than 19 of the class have been preserved following withdrawal. Notice the old water tank in the background, a left-over from the days of steam. *Brian Jackson*

Below: **EXETER ST DAVID'S** Although a station on this site was first opened in 1844 by the Bristol & Exeter Railway, most of the buildings seen in this photograph date from the 1864 rebuild, and were designed by Francis Fox. A Bristol VR bus operated by Devon General provides a convenient rail/bus interchange; by 1983 Devon General was part of Western National and its buses were painted in National Bus Company green rather than the once familiar Devon General maroon. The city centre is a considerable walk from the station. An interesting feature of Exeter St David's is that it is possible to catch a train to London in either direction; trains to Paddington leave the station in a northbound direction, while trains to Waterloo initially head southbound before turning east to climb the steep bank to Exeter Central. *Brian Jackson*

Above: **EXETER ST DAVID'S** Class 45 diesel-electric locomotive No 45042 enters Exeter St David's station on Thursday 11 August with an empty return working of china clay wagons. This locomotive was built at British Railways Crewe Works and entered traffic in June 1963 as No D57; it was withdrawn in April 1985 and subsequently scrapped. Notice the lower-quadrant signals and the goods shed in the background, while in the left foreground is Exeter Middle Signal Box, built in 1915 to a classic Great Western design adapted to fit the confined available space. *Brian Jackson*

1983 Arrivals & Departures

Births

Sean Biggerstaff	Actor		15 March
Bruno Langley	Actor		21 March
Simon Burnett	Swimmer		14 April
Matt Cardle	Singer		15 April
Natalie Cassidy	Actress		13 May
Jennifer Ellison	Actress		30 May
Lee Ryan	Singer		17 June
Cheryl Cole	Singer		30 June
Rory Jennings	Actor		20 July
Chantelle Houghton	Model		21 August
Christopher Parker	Actor		24 August
Amy Winehouse	Singer/songwriter	(d2011)	14 September
Harry Lloyd	Actor		17 November
Lucy Pinder	Model		20 December

Deaths

Fred Bakewell	Cricketer	(b1908)	23 January
Billy Fury	Singer/songwriter	(b1940)	28 January
Karen Carpenter	Musician	(b1950)	4 February
Sir Adrian Boult	Conductor	(b1889)	22 February
Sir William Walton	Composer	(b1902)	8 March
Jimmy Bloomfield	Footballer/manager	(b1934)	3 April
Gerry Hitchens	Footballer	(b1934)	13 April
Kenneth Clark	Art historian	(b1903)	21 May
David Niven	Actor	(b1910)	19 July
Ralph Richardson	Actor	(b1902)	10 October
John Le Mesurier	Actor	(b1912)	15 November
Richard Llewellyn	Writer	(b1906)	30 November
Mary Renault	Writer	(b1905)	13 December
Colin Middleton	Artist	(b1910)	23 December

BARNSTAPLE Until 1970 this station was called Barnstaple Junction, Barnstaple Town being the next station on the line to Ilfracombe. This photograph, showing a three-car DMU forming the 1221 departure to Exeter St David's on Monday 8 August, conveys an atmosphere of faded grandeur, and indeed the station had known much better days. Twenty years previously it had been a significant junction, but the closure to passengers of the line to Bideford and Torrington in 1965, followed by the complete closure of the lines to Dulverton and Taunton in 1966 and the line onwards to Barnstaple Town and Ilfracombe in 1970 resulted in only the route to Exeter St David's serving this location.

An encouraging development in more recent years has been the opening, in August 2008, of a café in the old station house – the Station Master's Special Full English Breakfast is highly recommended! – bringing back into use this interesting building designed by Sir William Tite and dating from 1854.

CHELFHAM VIADUCT Opened in May 1898, the Lynton & Barnstaple Railway was a 2-foot-gauge line that ran 19 miles from a bay platform at Barnstaple Town station to a terminus at Lynton. The principal engineering structure on the line was Chelfham (pronounced 'Chillham') Viaduct; the eight spans, each 42 feet wide, carry the line about 70 feet above the Stoke Rivers valley. The cost of construction was around £6,500 and the viaduct required more than 250,000 bricks. The line was bought by the Southern Railway in 1923 and investment included re-ballasting the track and refurbishment of the passenger carriages, together with improved publicity. However, although the line was popular with holidaymakers, very few local people used it after highway improvements and the coming of motor vehicles offered quicker journeys by road. The line was running at a considerable loss, and was

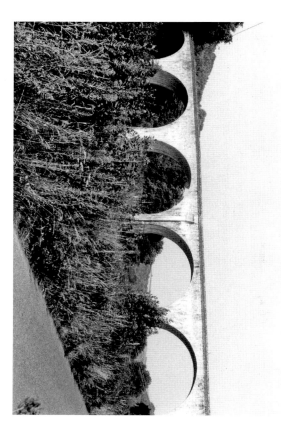

closed in September 1935. Nonetheless, much of the trackbed and many of the buildings and structures survive; Chelfham Viaduct was photographed on Monday 8 August 1983.

LYNTON On the day after the line closed, a wreath left at Barnstaple Town station was accompanied by a card that read 'Perchance it is not dead, but sleepeth'. The line slept for a very long time, but in the mid-1990s Woody Bay station was acquired by preservationists, and after years of work on restoration and track-laying the first trains on a restored portion of the route ran in the summer of 2004. At the time of writing trains run between Woody Bay station and Killington Lane Halt on operating days – a round trip of 2 miles – and there are plans to restore more of the route in stages. The stations at Lynton, Woody Bay and Blackmoor were all built in the same distinctive style and all survive. This photograph, also taken on Monday 8 August 1983, illustrates the erstwhile Lynton station, at that time externally very similar to its appearance when the line closed – this building is currently a private residence and is not part of the restored railway, so there is no public access.

LYNTON Beautifully situated on the rugged North Devon coast, the twin towns of Lynton and Lynmouth have long been popular with visitors. However, the high cliffs dividing the two towns were starting to cause problems by the middle of the 19th century. The remote and rugged nature of the area made it economically sensible to delivery many of life's essentials, such as coal and foodstuffs, by sea to Lynmouth; these goods then had to be hauled up the very steep hill to Lynton. A worthwhile tourist trade was developing as paddle steamers from Bristol and Swansea visited Lynmouth, but day trippers who decided to walk up to Lynton were faced with a significant gradient.

Work to build the Lynton & Lynmouth Cliff Railway started in 1887. The railway was designed by George Marks, and was largely financed by publisher Sir George Newnes (who also backed the Lynton & Barnstaple Railway). The construction work was overseen by local builder Bob Jones. The railway has parallel tracks 862 feet long at a gauge of 3ft 9in and rises 500 feet at a gradient of 1 in 1.72. Using entirely manual labour, the building of the railway was completed in less than three years, and the link between the twin towns was opened on Easter Monday, 7 April 1890.

The two cars on the railway are connected by cables that run around pulleys at the upper and lower stations. Underneath each car is a 700-gallon tank containing water piped from the West Lyn River. When the cars are stationary with full tanks at each end of the line, they are, effectively, balanced. When the driver of the lower car lets water out of the tank, this makes the top car heavier, and it therefore descends while pulling the lower car up the railway.

This photograph, taken on Monday 8 August 1983, is looking down the railway from a descending car; notice how the sets of rails part slightly to allow the two cars to pass safely at the centre of the incline. Given that the lifts run solely on water and need absolutely no power to operate, the Lynton & Lynmouth Cliff Railway has to be the easiest and most environmentally friendly way to travel between the twin towns.

OKEHAMPTON For many years Okehampton was a significant station on the former LSWR route between Exeter and Plymouth, portions of trains running to and from Padstow and Bude being detached or attached here. Service patterns were revised in 1964, and passenger services from Okehampton to Halwill, and thence to Padstow and Bude, were withdrawn in October 1966. A further blow came in May 1968 when the route between Okehampton and Bere Alston was closed to passengers, severing the route to Plymouth. Okehampton station remained open, served from Exeter, but this service was withdrawn in June 1972, although the line from Yeoford through Sampford Courtenay and Okehampton to Meldon Quarry remained open for ballast trains. Photographed on Tuesday 2 August 1983, looking towards Meldon, the station looks remarkably complete considering that regular passenger services had ceased 11 years previously.

OKEHAMPTON Looking towards Exeter from the station footbridge, a Class 33 diesel-electric locomotive heads towards Meldon Quarry with a train of return empty stone wagons. In 1997 Devon County Council, keen to encourage the use of public transport by Sunday visitors to Dartmoor, sponsored a passenger service between Exeter and Okehampton on summer Sundays. This has continued in subsequent years, while heritage services are now also based at Okehampton, the station having been beautifully restored in Southern Region colours, including an excellent buffet under the auspices of the Dartmoor Railway Supporters Association – it is well worth a visit. Since 2008 the Dartmoor Railway has been owned by British American Railway Services; the future operation of heritage services was under consideration at the time of going to press.

Below: **BERE ALSTON** Originally a station on the LSWR route to Plymouth, Bere Alston became a junction when a branch to Callington was opened in 1908. The branch was slated for closure in the Beeching Report; however, largely because the geography of the area precludes easy access to Plymouth by road from some to the communities served, the branch was reprieved, although truncated to terminate at Gunnislake. Thus Bere Alston station on the former Waterloo-Exeter-Plymouth main line remains open, although this photograph taken on Saturday 6 August 1983 illustrates that the premises had clearly seen better days. The view is looking towards Plymouth, and despite the 'Plymouth' destination display the two-car Class 118 DMU is forming the 1130 service to Gunnislake; it will reverse here at Bere Alston to run onto the former Callington branch.

Above: **GUNNISLAKE** The Callington branch was cut short to terminate at Gunnislake from 7 November 1966. When this photograph was taken in 1983 only the up side of what had been a through island platform was in use; cars can be seen on the right of the photograph parked in the area previously occupied by the down line. By this time the quaint buildings that had been in the centre of the platform, and which had survived painted in Southern Region colours until the late 1970s, had been demolished and replaced by a rather featureless concrete shelter (visible in front of the parked cars). The two-car Class 118 DMU, built by the Birmingham Railway Carriage & Wagon Company in 1960, will form the 1733 service to Plymouth on Saturday 6 August; it is pleasing to note that a good number of passengers have alighted from the terminating service. In 1994 Gunnislake station was moved from this site, slightly shortening the remaining branch, in order to eliminate a very low bridge over the A390 road.

Below: **PLYMOUTH** The main station at Plymouth is situated north of the city centre, and was called Plymouth North Road until the old LSWR terminus station at Plymouth Friary closed in 1958. The GWR had commenced a rebuilding scheme at Plymouth North Road in 1938, but work was deferred as a result of the Second World War, and much of the present structure was built between 1956 and 1962; the refurbished station was formally opened by Dr Beeching on 26 March in the later year. Class 45 locomotive No 45037 was photographed while shunting at Plymouth station on Saturday 6 August 1983. Built at BR Derby Works and entering service as No D46 in October 1961, No 45037 remained in active service with British Rail until July 1988.

Above: **DEVONPORT** There are three operating bases for the Royal Navy in Britain: Portsmouth, Faslane and Devonport. The Devonport Dockyard was once the home of a remarkable railway system, tracks having been laid in the North Yard in 1860 and through the tunnel connecting the North and South Yards in 1876. From the opening of the Extension Yard in the early years of the 20th century, the Dockyard Railway ran a passenger service in order to convey naval and dockyard workers between the yards, and this continued until 1966. However, the railway was mostly used for freight, including steel plate for shipbuilding. Power was by steam locomotives until the first diesels were introduced in the mid-1950s, one of which was this Hibbert Planet shunter, No 5199, new in 1955 and photographed awaiting its next turn of duty early in 1983. The line through the tunnel linking the North and South Yards closed in 1982, but railway continues in use in the North Yard in the 21st century. *Brian Jackson*

Left: **ST ERTH** Opened by the West Cornwall Railway as St Ives Road in March 1852, this station was renamed St Erth when a branch line to the resort of St Ives was opened in June 1877. This photograph was taken from the east end of the up platform looking towards Hayle; the branch to St Ives can be seen curving away to the left – notice also the spur connecting the branch to the main line. The platform for branch-line trains to St Ives is behind the fence on the left; it is at a slightly lower level and is reached by a couple of steps down from the main-line platform. The signal box in the background dates from 1899. Class 46 locomotive No 46027, built by BR Derby Works and entering service as No D164 in April 1962, was shunting china clay hoppers into the sidings when photographed on Wednesday 3 August 1983; it was withdrawn in November 1984 and subsequently scrapped.

Right: **PENZANCE** Now the next station down the line from St Erth, since the intermediate station at Marazion sadly closed in October 1964. Penzance is the final station in Cornwall. A great place to watch the trains here is looking over the wall from Chyandour Cliff. Ray Ruffell photographed the scene from here on Wednesday 3 August. A rake of air-conditioned stock with a Mark 1 catering car awaits a locomotive in Platform 2, but of greater interest is the Travelling Post Office train being loaded at Platform 4 on the far side of the station; in the distance a Royal Mail van has reversed against the side of the stock. The train is headed by Class 45 locomotive No 45150, built by BR Crewe Works as No D78 and in service from December 1960 until February 1988. Sadly, this is an operation that will not be seen any more; after a long history the last Travelling Post Office trains ran on Britain's railway network in January 2004.

Wales Walkabout

CARDIFF CENTRAL was opened by the South Wales Railway in 1850 and was completely rebuilt by the GWR in 1932; the concourse retains some art deco features and on the exterior of the building 'Great Western Railway' remains carved in large letters above the main entrance. The station was known as Cardiff General until 1973. InterCity 125 High Speed Trains started to operate on the London-Cardiff-Swansea route from October 1976, offering a much faster service than hitherto, and were marketed as 'the changing face of rail'. In the first two years of HST operation ridership on the route increased by 33%. On Bank Holiday Monday, 30 May 1983, HST unit No 253015 pauses at Cardiff Central while working the 1230 service from Swansea to London Paddington.

In contrast, Class 33 diesel-electric No 33052, with a rake of 1950s-design BR Standard Mark I carriages on a Bank Holiday working from Cardiff to Crewe, illustrates a more traditional railway scene that was still in evidence in 1983. The Class 33 locomotives were built by the Birmingham Railway Carriage & Wagon Company for the Southern Region, and No 33052 entered service in 1961 as No D6570, spending most of its life allocated to Hither Green depot. Having been renumbered under the TOPS scheme, it was given the name *Ashford* at Ashford station on 15 May 1980. Withdrawn in February 1997, the locomotive has been preserved on the Kent & East Sussex Railway under its original number and in original green livery, although the name *Ashford* has been retained.

Below: **CARDIFF DOCKS** The Queen Alexandra Dock was the last to be built and the largest of Cardiff's docks, being opened by His Majesty King Edward VII on 13 July 1907. Beside an impressive line of dockside cranes, Class 08 diesel shunter No 08780 is shunting at Queen Alexandra Dock on Monday 12 December 1983. In all, 966 of this class were built, and they were a very familiar sight throughout British Railways. This example was constructed at BR Derby Works as No D3948 and entered traffic in April 1960; it was to clock up almost 45 years of service before withdrawal in March 2005.

Below right: **CARDIFF PIERHEAD** Railway signals controlling train movements on swing bridges crossing docks or rivers were not uncommon, but these arrangements at Cardiff Pierhead, to control shipping movements, are very unusual. Sadly, by the time this photograph was taken in April 1983 the great days of shipping had passed, and no longer did the graceful paddle steamers of P. & A. Campbell enter Cardiff on their cruises of the Bristol Channel. *Brian Jackson*

Right: **CARDIFF** The Welsh Industrial & Maritime Museum at Cardiff opened in 1977 and was located in an area of Cardiff Docks that was then in decline; it closed at this location in 1998 when the site was cleared as part of the Cardiff Bay redevelopment. Exhibited at the museum in April 1983 was Hudswell Clark 0-6-0 saddle tank No 544 of 1900 vintage, which had formerly been employed by the National Coal Board at Coed Ely. After closure, the exhibits were transferred to other venues, No 544 in due course going to the Big Pit Mining Museum at Blaenavon. *Brian Jackson*

Below: **NEWPORT** Transporter bridges are a way of crossing a river without impeding navigation, but there were very few in the British Isles. This example on the River Usk at Newport was opened

in September 1906. Winding a cable around a drum in the motor house pulled the gondola across the river at a maximum speed of 10 feet per second. The bridge was featured in the 1959 film *Tiger Bay* starring Hayley Mills and her father John Mills, although to suit the purpose of the story its location was made out to be Cardiff Docks. The bridge is seen here in operation on Wednesday 13 April 1983. Now a listed structure, this interesting piece of transport history is owned and operated by Newport City Council, although during the 21st century most motor traffic crosses the River Usk by the new bridge that was opened a little further upstream in 2005. *Brian Jackson*

CAERPHILLY In 1963 the former Rhymney Railway Company's works at Caerphilly was disposed of by British Railways, the site becoming an industrial estate. One of the buildings was bought by South Wales Switchgear, and some railway enthusiasts employed by the company formed a group that was to become the origins of the Caerphilly Railway Society. The group obtained permission to build a short platform beside the remaining track and to erect a signal box that had previously been at Rhiwderin station. They also commenced the restoration of an interesting steam locomotive, which was delivered to Caerphilly in 1967. This Class 2 0-6-2 mixed-traffic loco was built by the Taff Vale Railway Company at West Yard Works, Cardiff, in 1897 and entered service as No 28. It passed to the Great Western Railway with the 1923 Grouping, but was withdrawn in 1926. Sold to the Longmoor Military Railway the following year, the locomotive remained in Hampshire until sold to South Hetton Colliery, County Durham, at the end of the Second World War. Withdrawn by the National Coal Board in 1960, TVR No 28 eventually returned to South Wales, and after restoration by members of the Caerphilly Railway Society was returned to steam in 1983; Ray Ruffell took these photographs during a visit on Monday 30 May.

In 1996 most members of the Caerphilly Railway Society moved to the Gwili Railway at Carmarthen, although TVR No 28 was transferred to the Dean Forest Railway, while the signal box from the Caerphilly site was moved to the Teifi Valley Railway in 1998.

Above: **WELSHPOOL** The Welshpool & Llanfair Railway opened in 1903, linking Welshpool with Llanfair Caereinion. It was built to a 2ft 6in gauge and included tight curves and steep gradients to minimise the cost of construction. The line was worked by the Cambrian Railways, then passed to the Great Western Railway with the 1923 Grouping. Passenger services were discontinued in 1931, but the line remained open for freight until November 1956. Preservationists were determined to restore services, and the first section to reopen was between Llanfair Caereinion and Castle Caereinion in April 1963. By 1972 the line had reopened to Sylfaen, and trains reached Raven Square, Welshpool, in July 1981. A feature of this line is the use of preserved narrow-gauge locomotives and stock from other countries, exemplified here at Welshpool on Friday 26 August 1983. The 0-8-0 tank locomotive was built in 1944 and was originally used by the German Army, then on the Zillertalbahn in the Austrian Tyrol before coming to the Welshpool & Llanfair Railway in 1969, where it was named *Sir Drefaldwyn*.

Below: **LLANGOLLEN** Built by the Llangollen & Corwen Railway Company in 1865 and refurbished and extended by the Great Western Railway in 1900, Llangollen station occupies a scenic location beside the River Dee; notice how the footbridge steps overhang the river. This photograph was taken in April 1983 and records the early days of the Llangollen Railway's restoration of part of the old main line between Ruabon and Barmouth, which had closed to passengers in 1965 and freight in 1968. An industrial diesel locomotive stands in the platform with two non-gangwayed BR Standard Mark I carriages and a brake van. Extensions to services on this line are ongoing; there are now a number of preserved steam locomotives in operation and at the time of writing it is projected that the line will be reopened to Corwen during the 2013 season. *Brian Jackson*

Left: **ABERYSTWYTH** It is an accepted fact that steam traction on British Rail finally ended in August 1968; there was, however, one exception – the narrow gauge line from Aberystwyth to Devil's Bridge in Wales. Opened in 1902, the line came under the control of the Cambrian Railways in 1912 and thus passed to the Great Western Railway in 1923. The passenger service became summer-only after the 1930 season, and the line closed completely during the Second World War; summer passenger services resumed in 1945 and the line was taken into British Railways ownership in 1948. The GWR had built three new steam locomotives for the line at Swindon Works in 1923, and in the 1970s – when these were the only steam-hauled services operated by British Rail – it was a strange experience to see them painted blue and sporting the 'double arrow' logo. However, when photographed in July 1983 No 9 *Prince of Wales* was sporting a yellow ochre livery. The Vale of Rheidol Railway was subsequently privatised in 1989. *Brian Jackson*

Right: **TYWYN** With a gauge of 2ft 3in and rising from the coast at Tywyn to a quarry at Abergynolwyn, 243 feet above sea level, the Talyllyn Railway in Wales was opened in 1866 primarily for the slate trade, although passenger services were also operated. The quarry and line were bought by Henry Haydn Jones MP in 1911, and the quarry closed in 1946, but the railway continued to run until Haydn Jones died in 1950. The future for the line then looked bleak, but fortunately a group of enthusiasts, led by writer and engineer L. T. C. Rolt, formed the Talyllyn Railway Preservation Society, which took over the operation of the line in 1951, when the Talyllyn became the first preserved railway in the UK. *Dolgoch*, an 0-4-0 well tank built by Fletcher Jennings in 1866, is still in operation on the line, and was photographed with its vintage train prior to departure for Abergynolwyn in June 1983. *Brian Jackson*

Left: **PRESTATYN** The original station here opened on 1 May 1848 when the Chester & Holyhead Railway Company's line was opened as far as Bangor; the line was completed to Holyhead two years later and became part of the London & North Western Railway in January 1859. The original station closed completely to both passenger and goods traffic on 22 February 1897 when the present station was opened a short distance to the west. Nonetheless, the original station and goods shed were still standing more than 85 years after closure when Class 25 diesel-electric locomotive No 25083 was photographed passing with a rake of BR Standard Mark I stock on Monday 11 April 1983. This locomotive was built at BR Derby Works and entered service in December 1963 as No D5233; withdrawn in July 1984, it has subsequently been preserved at the Caledonian Railway, Brechin, Scotland. *Brian Jackson*

Right: **LLANERCH-Y-MOR** In a situation that could be described as 'up the creek', former British Railways Irish Sea ferry *Duke of Lancaster* was photographed beached at Llanerch-y-mor, off the River Dee near Mostyn, North Wales, in April 1983. Built in 1956, this fine ship was used on the Heysham-Belfast route, and provided a very high standard of accommodation for passengers. In 1975 she became a reserve vessel at Holyhead, and was subsequently sold and moved to Llanerch-y-mor in August 1979. It was intended that she would become a static leisure centre and market called The Fun Ship, but sadly – as with a number of such ventures – success was short-lived and, despite a number of efforts to revive the project, by 2013 disuse had brought deterioration to this once proud vessel. *Brian Jackson*

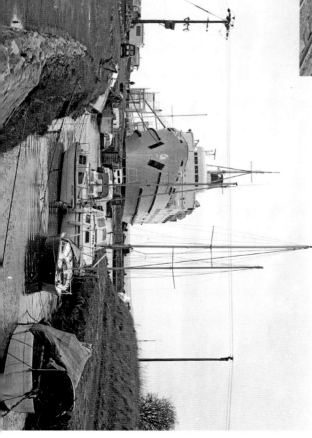

Catch it while you can: the Weymouth Harbour Tramway

WEYMOUTH The Weymouth Harbour Tramway was an unusual arrangement; although classed as a tramway, main-line trains proceeded along it for a mile through the streets of Weymouth in order to reach Weymouth Quay station and the Channel Islands steamers. The line had no signalling nor locking of the facing points – detailed special working arrangements ensured that two trains never met on this unique line. On Thursday 3 March 1983 a Western Region DMU makes a trial run along the tramway to ensure that the route will be suitable for through boat trains from Bristol during the coming summer. *Brian Jackson*

WEYMOUTH A further trial was carried out on the tramway that day, with the stock of the South Western Travelling Post Office being used to make up the load. This was the first recorded occasion that mail vans had traversed the tramway; be that as it may, the postman on his bicycle, seen on the right, appears completely oblivious of the event. *Brian Jackson*

Right: **WEYMOUTH** History was made on Tuesday 8 March when two car-carrying trains brought 105 new Metro and Mini cars from Birmingham to Weymouth Quay for shipping to the Channel Islands. A sea mist has descended as a Class 33 diesel-electric locomotive propels the second train into the platform at Weymouth Quay station. This once-only working was not repeated, as a later consignment of cars for the Channel Islands was unloaded at the town station and driven to the harbour. *Brian Jackson*

Below: **WEYMOUTH** During its last few years of operation a number of enthusiasts' railtours visited the tramway. One such was the Hertfordshire Rail Tours 'Thames Piddle Executive' on Saturday 19 March 1983. The train was formed of 'Hastings'

DEMUs Nos 1017 and 1032; it started from Watford Junction and visited Ludgershall, Fawley, Bournemouth West Sidings and Furzebrook, as well as the Weymouth Harbour Tramway. The railtour was photographed passing under Town Bridge alongside Weymouth Harbour. Notice the 12ft 6in height restriction sign for the bridge and the dip in the line to allow clearance, as well as the 'Road liable to flooding' sign, which could happen under the bridge at high spring tides. *Brian Jackson*

WEYMOUTH In July 1983 a Class 33 diesel-electric locomotive waits at Weymouth Quay station ready to depart for London Waterloo, complete with a 'Channel Islands Boat Train' headboard and showing the '90' headcode carried by these workings. On the left a Western Region DMU waits to depart for Bristol via Yeovil, Westbury and Bath. Time was running out for these workings; the last boat train to use the tramway ran on 26 September 1987, although Weymouth Quay station, which had been rebuilt in the 1960s to the form seen here, still stands and in the 21st century is used as office accommodation by Condor Ferries. *Brian Jackson*

1983 Happenings (2)

July
- Former Prime Minister Harold Wilson is given life peerage.
- Ford Orion compact saloon enters production.

August
- Car registrations start using letter prefixes – logically starting with A for the first year.

September
- Ian MacGregor becomes Chairman of National Coal Board.
- SDP Conference votes against merger with Liberal Party.
- Establishment of an Enterprise Zone of the Isle of Dogs in East London marks start of Docklands redevelopment.
- In a mass breakout, 38 IRA detainees escape from Maze Prison, Ulster.

October
- Neil Kinnock is elected leader of Labour Party.
- At a CND march in London, more than a million people demonstrate against nuclear weapons.

November
- Multiple killer Dennis Nilsen (see page 14) is sentenced to life imprisonment.
- First US cruise missiles arrive at RAF Greenham Common.
- Janet Walton gives birth to girl sextuplets in Liverpool.
- At London Heathrow Airport 6,800 gold bars worth almost £26 million are stolen from Brinks-MAT vault.

December
- First heart and lung transplant operation in Britain is carried out at Harefield Hospital.
- House of Lords votes to allow its debates to be broadcast on television.
- On the 17th a car bomb planted by Provisional IRA outside Harrods in London kills six people and injures 90; it is followed up on Christmas Day with further bomb in London, in Oxford Street – fortunately there are no casualties this time.

The Heart of England

Below: **LEDBURY** A three-car DMU forming the 1230 service from Birmingham to Hereford arrives at Ledbury on Friday 11 March. Ledbury station opened in 1861, and the signal box seen on the right dates from 1885. Just visible in the background is the entrance to the single-track Ledbury Tunnel; at 1,323 yards long, it was unpopular with locomotive crews in steam days owing to the particularly narrow bore and the gradient of 1 in 80. An unusual feature of Ledbury station in the 21st century is the privately run ticket office; this occupies a wooden chalet located on part of the site of the former main station building, which regrettably has long been demolished.

Above: **BROMSGROVE** With a gradient of 1 in 37, the 2-mile Lickey Incline is the steepest sustained main-line railway gradient in England. In steam days many trains needed banking assistance to tackle this formidable gradient, and in 1919 the Midland Railway built a special 0-10-0 steam locomotive, No 2290, at Derby Works particularly for this duty. Known as 'Big Bertha', it was used for this task until 1956, when the main banking loco became BR Standard 9F No 92079. In later years 'Hymek' diesel locomotives with specially modified transmissions were used. Looking towards Birmingham, Bromsgrove station stands at the foot of the notorious incline. On Saturday 4 June 1983 Class 50 diesel-electric locomotive No 50011, in service with British Rail from March 1968 until February 1987, rushes off the incline and through the station with a North East to South West inter-regional train. In the 21st century the ascent of the Lickey Incline is scarcely noticed when travelling in the 'Voyager' cross-country units that form the express services on this route.

TV Favourites

Breakfast Time
It was on Monday 17 January 1983 that breakfast television was first seen on our screens when this new programme, initially introduced by Frank Bough and Selina Scott, started transmission.

Good Morning Britain
Two weeks later ITV also started a breakfast-time current affairs programme made by TV-am.

Blockbusters
'Can I have a P please, Bob?' The quiz programme for young people, presented by Bob Holness, was first broadcast by ITV in 1983.

Death of an Expert Witness
Made by Anglia Television, this was the first of its dramatisations of the brilliant detective novels by P. D. James. Roy Marsden starred as the cultured detective Adam Dalgliesh.

Just Good Friends
This light-hearted comedy series was first seen in September 1983. Vince, a 'Jack the lad' character (played by Paul Nicholas) chances to meet Penny (played by Jan Francis), the rather uptight middle-class girl he had jilted a few years previously. Over the next few series the romance rekindles, and the couple eventually get married.

Auf Wiedersehen, Pet
A group of Geordie building workers take work in Germany in this comedy drama that soon became extremely popular.

The Black Adder
Initially set in medieval Britain, this comedy starred Rowan Atkinson and later became *Blackadder* for series 2-4, each being set in a different era.

KINGSWINFORD JUNCTION SOUTH SIGNAL BOX

Located near the site of the former Brierley Hill station (closed in 1962), and photographed in November 1983, Kingswinford Junction South Signal Box was a variation of a design first introduced by the Great Western Railway in 1896, but constructed in timber instead of brick. It was equipped with a 77-lever three-bar vertical tappet frame dating back to 1924. Sadly the box was destroyed by fire after an arson attack in November 2001; it was replaced by an industrial steel container to house the instruments and an open 11-lever ground frame, the site surrounded by a steel security fence. *Brian Jackson*

Right: **TYSELEY** Built at Swindon Works, 'Castle' Class locomotive No 7029 *Clun Castle* entered service in May 1950. When withdrawn in December 1965 it was the last 'Castle' locomotive in the British Railways fleet, having had the distinction of hauling the last scheduled steam-hauled service to depart from London Paddington, and also the last steam passenger train from the old Birmingham Snow Hill station. Preserved after withdrawal, *Clun Castle* was the first locomotive to come to what became the Standard Gauge Steam Trust at Tyseley, West Midlands, where it is seen during an open day giving rides to visitors in a BR Standard Mark I carriage on Sunday 6 November 1983. In the 21st century Tyseley is the centre of operations for Vintage Trains, operating the 'Shakespeare Express' and other railtours that offer the chance to enjoy traditional-style train travel – including the option of premier dining. There are still open days at Tyseley on occasion, allowing visitors to see behind the scenes; at the time of writing *Clun Castle* is undergoing further restoration, with a projected completion date of 2014.

Left: **DUDLEY** Opened in the late 1970s, the fascinating Black Country Museum brings to life the industrial heritage of the West Midlands; the site now covers 26 acres and is one of the finest and largest open-air museums in the United Kingdom. Photographed on Tuesday 12 April 1983, this single-deck tram dates from 1920 and operated on the 3ft 6in-gauge lines of the Dudley, Stourbridge & District Electric Traction Company. When the Stourbridge route was abandoned in 1930 the body of this tram became a garden summer house, but was acquired for preservation in the 1970s and restoration was completed by 1980.

WELLINGBOROUGH An InterCity 125 HST unit forming the 0905 service from Sheffield to London St Pancras runs into Wellingborough station on Saturday 23 April 1983. Opened in 1857, for many years this station was called Wellingborough Midland to avoid confusion with Wellingborough London Road station on the Northampton to Peterborough line, which closed to passengers in May 1964. The signal box seen here dates from 1893 and replaced an earlier box that had been located on the down side of the line. It is of Midland Railway Type 2b design, and was extended in 1915 to accommodate a 48-lever frame. The screen on the white post just to the left of the signal box steps is an illuminated panel that indicates whether or not it is safe to cross the line using the barrow crossing. This signal box was closed in December 1987 and subsequently demolished.

WELLINGBOROUGH On the same day, Ray Ruffell also took time to visit the Wagon Repairs Limited's facility which was to be found to the north of the station. Wagon Repairs Ltd was formed in Rotherham as far back as March 1918. The business developed a national network of repair facilities with depots in many locations including Stoke on Trent, Lydney, Radstock, Bristol, Cardiff, Barry, Bridgend and Swansea. The Wellingborough works closed during this year and Ray was presumably keen to capture the scene while there was still time. The works numbers of the two Ruston Hornsby locomotives were not recorded by Ray but one proudly carries a nameplate, presumably presented by members of the workforce - no doubt there is a story behind this yet to be discovered by your author.

SPONDON The origins of Spondon can be traced back to the Domesday Book of 1086. The village was absorbed as a suburb of Derby in 1968, although something of a village feel remains in places. Spondon station was opened in June 1839, and in this photograph, taken on Wednesday 26 October 1983, a three-car DMU is passing forming the 1120 Crewe to Lincoln service. The Class 120 power cars were built at British Railways Swindon Works in the late 1950s; in this unit the centre trailer carriage has been replaced by a Class 101 Metropolitan-Cammell trailer of similar vintage. In the 21st century, although Spondon station remains open, most local passenger traffic between there and Derby uses the Spondon Flyer bus service operated by Trent Barton, with high-quality specially branded vehicles and providing, at the time of writing, a bus every 10 minutes on weekdays during the daytime and every 30 minutes at evenings and on Sundays.

NOTTINGHAM Class 120 DMU stock was also used for the Branch Line Society's 'Wyvern Express' railtour on Saturday 23 April. Having started from Leicester, the train is seen, complete with headboard, on the right; the tour had just visited Nottingham Carriage Sidings and was taking a booked 45-minute break at Nottingham station before proceeding to Butterley (see opposite). On the left Class 45 diesel-electric locomotive No 45131, in service with British Rail from October 1961 until September 1986, hauls a rake of air-conditioned stock forming the 1235 service from Sheffield to London St Pancras. Formerly known as Nottingham Midland, at the time of writing Nottingham station is undergoing extensive refurbishment scheduled for completion in 2014.

BUTTERLEY

After departing from Nottingham, the 'Wyvern Express' railtour continued via Trowell Junction and Codnor Park Junction to Butterley. This is located on the old Pye Bridge to Ambergate line; passenger services had been withdrawn in June 1947 and the line closed completely in 1968. When the Midland Railway Trust came to the site in 1973 it had to more or less start from scratch; the former station at Butterley had been demolished, but the station building from Whitwell in South Derbyshire was moved and rebuilt at Butterley, while the extensive collection of historic transport-related artefacts now displayed at nearby Swanwick Junction is worth travelling many miles to see. Back in April 1983 the 'Wyvern Express' is about to pass Fowler 4F No 4027; it appears that the latter's crew have just returned the compliment by photographing the railtour train. No 4027 had been built at Derby Works and was in service for 40 years, from November 1924 until November 1964; at the time of writing it is located on the Gloucestershire Warwickshire Railway. Note the grounded carriage body on the right, a former Pullman coach dating back to 1874.

Used for shunting and also light freight and passenger duties, the LMS took into stock a total of 422 3F 0-6-0T locomotives between 1924 and 1930, which were commonly known as 'Jinties'. This example is being admired by passengers from the 'Wyvern Express'; it was built by the North British Locomotive Company, Glasgow, and entered traffic in July 1926. After withdrawal in December 1966 it was bought from Woodham's scrapyard at Barry in 1970 by the Midland Railway Trust and had the distinction of being the very last steam locomotive to be overhauled at BR Derby Works – and has a 1973 rebuilding plate on the front splasher. When withdrawn from BR service this locomotive carried the number 47357; here it carries the number 16440, which it had never carried while in traffic.

Meandering on Merseyside

Below: **BIRKENHEAD NORTH** When opened by the Wirral Railway in 1878 this station was known as Birkenhead Docks; the Wirral Railway was subsequently absorbed into the LMS, and the station was renamed Birkenhead North in 1926. The former Wirral Railway lines through Birkenhead North to West Kirby and New Brighton were electrified in 1938, and sets of very comfortable and well-appointed multiple units were provided to operate the services. However, time was running out for the 1938 units when this photograph was taken on Sunday 10 April 1983. Sets of Class 508 EMUs originally built for the Southern Region were being transferred to work on the Wirral lines; they were virtually identical to the Class 507 units that had replaced older trains on the third-rail electrified lines north of the River Mersey from the late 1970s onwards. A recently transferred Class 508 unit is seen on the right of this photograph. Around 20 of these units had been transferred north by the summer of 1983, all had arrived by December 1984, and the last of the 1938 LMS-type units was withdrawn in March 1985. *Brian Jackson*

Above: **LIVERPOOL PIER HEAD** In 1965 *Ferry 'Cross the Mersey* by Gerry and the Pacemakers reached No 8 in the UK singles chart, but the subject of this popular song is a vital form of transport for many inhabitants of both Liverpool and the Wirral area. On Sunday 10 April 1983 MV *Mountwood*, launched in 1959, waits at the Liverpool landing stage before sailing for Birkenhead. In 2002 she underwent a major refit, including new engines, and her name was also changed to *Royal Iris of the Mersey*. *Brian Jackson*

Right: **SOUTHPORT** During the later years of the 19th century Southport had three railway termini: Central (closed to passengers in May 1901, but continued in use as a goods depot until the 1970s), Lord Street (closed to passengers in January 1952 and to goods six months later), and Chapel Street, which remains in use, now known simply as Southport. As an aside, the closure of Lord Street for railway purposes was not the end of that building's role in passenger transport – it later served as Southport bus station for Ribble until the 1980s. This photograph was taken on Sunday 10 April 1983 and is looking towards the platforms and buffer-stops of the surviving Southport station, which is the terminus for trains from Liverpool and from Manchester via Wigan. *Brian Jackson*

Left: **SOUTHPORT** The Lakeside Miniature Railway has a long history. The initial half-mile of 15-inch-gauge line was opened in May 1911, and was extended at both ends in 1948 to operate for about three-quarters of a mile from Pleasureland to Peter Pan's Pool. Late-season holidaymakers are seen enjoying a ride on Saturday 24 September 1983; the train is hauled by diesel locomotive *Princess Anne*, which was built by Severn Lamb in 1971 to the outline of the BR Western Region 'Western' Class diesel-hydraulics; at the time of the photograph this was the newest locomotive on the line.

SOUTHPORT A visit to 'Steamport' at Southport on Sunday 10 April 1983 revealed an eclectic mix of exhibits including both steam and diesel locomotives, steam-rollers, a trolleybus, Liverpool trams and other items of transport interest, all housed in the former Southport motive power depot. This was a popular attraction during the 1980s, but during the following decade heavy repairs were found to be needed to the building, while the town-centre location meant that the running line at the site was short and there was no possibility of expansion. Sadly the Steamport collection was dispersed and the site has since been redeveloped. Locomotives on view on 10 April included Class 24 diesel-electric No 24081, which had been built at BR Crewe Works and entered traffic in March 1960 as No D5081; preserved after withdrawal in October 1980, at the time of writing it can be found at the Gloucestershire Warwickshire Railway.

Representing the smaller end of industrial locomotives was Sentinel shunter No 8024, constructed in 1929 for Cambridge Gas Works, where it had rejoiced in the name of *Gasbag*. The removal of the front panels reveals the small vertical steam engine that powered the machine, the boiler being contained in the section between this engine and the cab. Together with a number of other exhibits that were at Steamport, *Gasbag* now resides at the Ribble Steam Railway & Museum at Preston Docks. *Both Brian Jackson*

Selection from Scotland

GLASGOW QUEEN STREET

The first station on this site adjoining George Square in Glasgow was opened by the Edinburgh & Glasgow Railway in February 1842. This undertaking was absorbed into the North British Railway in 1865, and Queen Street station was rebuilt and enlarged in 1878. The remarkable roof over the platforms dates from this rebuild; 259 feet wide, 450 feet long and almost 79 feet above rail level at its highest point, it was designed by James Carswell, Chief Engineer of the North British Railway. Queen Street station is at the foot of the Cowlairs incline, well over a mile long and with a maximum gradient of 1 in 42, the half-mile closest to the station being in tunnel. Cable haulage of trains was used until 1908. Next to the station in George Square some elegant town houses dating from 1807 were converted for hotel use in 1878; the Hotel was later acquired by the North British Railway and, proudly renamed as the North British Hotel, Glasgow, in due course became part of the British Transport Hotels portfolio. Sadly that excellent railway hotel chain was broken up and privatised in the 1980s, and the North British was sold in 1984.

A listed building since 1970, it now operates as the Millennium Hotel and still provides comfortable and convenient accommodation for rail travellers. In the late 1960s/early 1970s some modernisation work was carried out at Queen Street station and additional accommodation was provided at the North British Hotel; in particular the entrance to the station from the street is now by a very 1970s-style shop/office building, but fortunately Carswell's historic roof was retained. Part of this can be seen in the photograph of Class 27 diesel-electric locomotive No 27054 at the buffer-stops with a rake of BR Standard Mark I stock on Friday 1 April 1983. Built by the Birmingham Railway Carriage & Wagon Company and entering service in July 1962 as No D5399, this locomotive was to see 25 years of service before withdrawal in July 1987.

The second photograph, taken from the outer end of the platforms, shows the deep cutting and the entrance to Cowlairs Tunnel. Class 37 diesel-electric locomotive No 37026 *Loch Awe* has a rake of steam-heated BR Standard Mark I stock forming the 1823 service to Oban. Built by English Electric Vulcan Foundry and in service from September 1961 until January 1999, this powerful locomotive will make easy work of the formidable incline.

STIRLING At the end of the 1970s it had been decided to upgrade the Glasgow Queen Street-Edinburgh Waverley service by introducing push-pull operation powered by a Class 47 locomotive in place of the pairs of Class 27 locomotives then employed on the route. To facilitate this, several British Rail Standard Mark 2f BSO carriages dating from 1974 were rebuilt at Glasgow Works to incorporate a driving cab at the brake van end; pulsed control signals were sent by a Time Division Multiplex (TDM) system through the carriage lighting control circuits. The converted driving trailer coaches could work with all air-braked stock to form push-pull trains with appropriately modified Class 47 diesel-electric locomotives (which were designated Class 47/7). Push-pull working took over the Glasgow-Edinburgh trains from February 1980 and was subsequently extended to Glasgow-Aberdeen services. The 1428 service from Perth to Glasgow enters Stirling station on Tuesday 5 April 1983; as was normal practice, the driving trailer carriage is at the Glasgow end of the train. Providing the motive power at the rear of the formation is Class 47 No 47701 (formerly No D1932).

No 1 Records

January
Save Your Love — Renée & Renato
You Can't Hurry Love — Phil Collins
Down Under — Men at Work

February
Too Shy — Kajagoogoo

March
Billie Jean — Michael Jackson
Total Eclipse of the Heart — Bonnie Tyler
Is There Something I Should Know — Duran Duran

April
Let's Dance — David Bowie

May
True — Spandau Ballet
Candy Girl — New Edition

June
Every Breath You Take — Police

July
Baby Jane — Rod Stewart
Wherever I Lay My Hat — Paul Young

August
Give It Up — KC & The Sunshine Band

September
Red Red Wine — UB40
Karma Chameleon — Boy George

October
Karma Chameleon — Boy George

November
Uptown Girl — Billy Joel

December
Only You — Flying Pickets

Below: **ABERDEEN** And so we end our tour of the British Rail network in 1983 at Aberdeen. The present station at this location was completed in 1916; it was a joint station for the Caledonian Railway and the Great North of Scotland Railway, designed by J. A. Parker and replacing an earlier structure on the same site that was no longer adequate for the growing level of traffic. A claim to fame for Aberdeen station is that it is the terminus of the longest through journey that it is possible to make on the UK rail network – the 770 miles to Penzance, which in the Cross Country timetable valid until 18 May 2013 departs from Aberdeen at 0820 on weekdays and arrives at Penzance at 2142. The InterCity 125 High Speed Train seen on Monday 4 April 1983 will form the 1030 departure for London King's Cross, a journey of 523 miles that will take 7 hours. On the left mail is ready to be loaded into the brake van section of the push-pull set that will form the next train to Glasgow.

Above: **INSCH** The date stone above the doorway confirms that the delightful station at Insch, on the line between Inverness and Aberdeen, was built in 1880; it replaced an earlier structure dating from 1854. It is good to see the survival of the station buildings; moreover, an encouraging number of people are waiting for the train on Monday 4 April 1983. Part of this station building has since become the Insch Connection Museum, which opened in December 1997. Now normally open between 1330 and 1700 on Wednesdays and Saturdays from April until October only, the museum contains many photographs and other items of local interest illustrating day-to-day life for the people of the Insch area in times gone by.

Index

LEDBURY In 1983 John Masefield School in Ledbury operated its own miniature railway within the grounds; the school continues to thrive in the 21st century, although sadly the miniature railway is no longer. Epitomising his interest in railways of all shapes and sizes, Ray Ruffell, attired in his British Rail uniform, is seen during a visit on Friday 11 March.